Kith and Kin

Kinship care for vulnerable yo

Bob Broad, Ruth Hayes and Christine Rushforth

JOSEPH
ROWNTREE
FOUNDATION

NATIONAL
CHILDREN'S
BUREAU

making a difference

The National Children's Bureau promotes the interests and well-being of all children and young people across every aspect of their lives. NCB advocates the participation of children and young people in all matters affecting them. NCB challenges disadvantage in childhood.

NCB achieves its mission by
- ensuring the views of children and young people are listened to and taken into account at all times
- playing an active role in policy development and advocacy
- undertaking high quality research and work from an evidence based perspective
- promoting multidisciplinary, cross-agency partnerships
- identifying, developing and promoting good practice
- disseminating information to professionals, policy makers, parents and children and young people

NCB has adopted and works within the UN Convention on the Rights of the Child.

Several Councils and Fora are based at NCB and contribute significantly to the breadth of its influence. It also works in partnership with Children in Scotland and Children in Wales and other voluntary organisations concerned for children and their families.

The Joseph Rowntree Foundation has supported this project as part of its programme of research and innovative development projects, which it hopes will be of value to policy makers and practitioners.

The views expressed in this book are those of the authors and not necessarily those of the National Children's Bureau or the Joseph Rowntree Foundation.

Published by National Children's Bureau Enterprises Ltd, the trading company for the National Children's Bureau, Registered Charity number 258825. 8 Wakley Street, London EC1V 7QE. Tel: 020 7843 6000

© National Children's Bureau and Joseph Rowntree Foundation, 2001
Published 2001

ISBN 1 900990 70 9

British Library Cataloguing in Publication Data
A catalogue record for this book is available from the British Library

Designed and typeset by Jeff Teader
Printed and bound by Page Bros, Norwich

Contents

List of figures

Acknowledgements

A large number of people enabled this project to take place. First and foremost we want to thank all the young people and carers who agreed to participate in the project. A special thanks is extended to the London Borough of Wandsworth Social Services Department for not only agreeing to be our partner in this research but subsequently providing help, support and assistance amid other more pressing priorities. The assistance of Wandsworth Social Services Department staff including Sally Watling and Joy Nield, and the professional guidance and enthusiasm of Fiona Wallace, Hilary Galloway and Alistair Hughes were especially welcome. We also want to acknowledge that throughout the research Wandsworth Social Services Department was very open to researchers accessing information and the subsequent critical assessment of their work as described in this report. A special thanks is extended to Denise Lawes, Senior Social Worker, London Borough of Wandsworth, who initially suggested kinship care as an area needing further research and development.

We would also like to thank the Joseph Rowntree Foundation for funding this research project and to Charlie Lloyd, Principal Research Manager at the Joseph Rowntree Foundation, for his capacity and skills in keeping the project focused and on track. A special thanks to the members of the project's Joseph Rowntree Foundation Advisory Group members, Dr Elaine Farmer, University of Bristol; Helen Jones, Department of Health; Alison Richards, Family Rights Group; Ann Wheal, University of Southampton; Joy Nield and Hilary Galloway, London Borough of Wandsworth Social Services Department; and Anthony Douglas, the Association of Directors of Social Services, for expert guidance.

We would particularly like to thank Lynda Ince, Royal Holloway College, University of London, who was project consultant on black perspectives, and Martin Clayton, of Clayton Reed Associates, for his input on the Statistical Package for the Social Sciences (SPSS) and statistical data, and for Clayton Reed Associates' valued expert support.

The project's secretarial work, including the painstaking transcription of the young people's taped interviews, was ably and speedily undertaken by Elizabeth Lightowler, Research Project Secretary, School of Health and Applied Social Sciences, De Montfort University. A thanks is also extended to Steve Allen, Wandsworth Safe Drug Agency, Age Concern (England), Wandsworth Age Concern and the Wandsworth Carers Centre.

Without all these people this project would not have been possible.

Bob Broad, School of Health and Applied Social Sciences, De Montfort University, Leicester
Ruth Hayes, Researcher
Christine Rushforth, Researcher

September 2001

Summary

This study is based on a sample of 50 young people in kinship care placements – that is, being looked after by relatives or friends with the knowledge of social services. Interviews were carried out with these young people, carers and social workers.

Findings

Young people

Forty-six of the 50 young people were aged between 14 and 25 years and the average age was 16.5 years. Nearly half of them were aged 16 or 17. Young people of Caribbean or Guyanese ethnic origin accounted for almost half the sample; around a third defined themselves as being of British ethnic origin.

Kinship carers

In all but one case, the ethnic origin of the kinship carer exactly matched that of the young person. Carers had an older age profile than either foster carers or the general parent population, with nearly three-quarters being over 50 years of age. Almost half of the carers were grandparents, nearly a quarter were aunts and the others were sisters, uncles, friends or cousins.

Ethnicity

Black young people and carers felt that kinship care was important in maintaining the young person's ethnic and cultural identity. Many of the families were mixed heritage.

Length of placement

Of the 39 placements where details were available, 20 had lasted almost continuously for between one and five years, 11 for over five years and 8 for less than one year.

The average length of placement was four years. While comparison is problematic, these kinship care placements appeared to be more stable and longer term than many alternatives.

Administrative categories

In 13 of the placements, payments were being made under Section 17 of the Children Act 1989; eight were on Residence Orders. However, in the majority of cases, the category was neither recorded nor known by the young person, carer or the young person's social worker. There is therefore a serious absence of legal and administrative clarity.

The four main routes into kinship care

1. A final resort for social services after other care options had failed.
2. A continuation of birth parent support already provided by the carer.
3. The first option for social services once the family situation had broken down.
4. An option selected by the young people themselves after a crisis at home.

The main reasons for young people living in kinship care

- Child protection issues, for example violence/abuse in family
- Inability of previous carer to cope, for example as a result of a death
- Young person's problems/difficult behaviour, for example offending/substance misuse.

Young people's views of kinship care

According to the young people the main *advantages* of kinship care were:
- feeling loved, valued and cared for
- belonging and feeling settled: not being moved around and subject to disruption, and being cared for and nurtured
- wanting to be with people who they know
- sustaining a sense of who they are (identity) through maintaining contact with family, siblings, and friends
- feeling safe from harm or threatening behaviour of adults (including in residential and foster care)
- being rescued from or not being sent into stranger local authority care
- being listened to.

The *limits* of kinship care for young people include:

- limitations to their freedom; for example wanting to have friends round or play music
- financial hardship resulting from insufficient payments for kinship care.

Kinship carers' views

- Carers were passionately in favour of kinship care for the following reasons: their love for the young person and (in the case of grandparents) love and desire to support the birth parent(s); the belief that family is the best place to raise young people; the desire to avoid the young person being placed in local authority care; and their belief that it supports a young person's sense of belonging, and racial and cultural heritage.
- Around half the carers reported few problems with young people's behaviour and there were examples of how carers helped the young people make dramatic improvements in their lifestyle. However the other half were struggling to cope with the difficult behaviour of the young people.
- Almost all carers believed that without their intervention the young person would have been placed in or returned to local authority care with damaging results.
- Almost all carers described drawbacks; the main ones were: shortage of money, loss of freedom and independence, overcrowding, problems relating to age and ill health, and problems relating to managing difficult behaviour.

Support for kinship care

- Calls for greater financial support and more consistent social work support and communication were almost universal. Carers wanted written information about financial support and specific grants available.
- Calls for certain specialist services were highly individual, emphasising the importance of comprehensive assessments of need leading to easier access to the different services in different departments, for example social services, health, education.
- The needs of some 17 and 18 year olds were for independent housing and more independent living and not for 'better' kinship care. This raises critical issues about how those young people make the transition to more independent living.

Policy/practice implications

- Policy and practice are both hampered by the ambiguity in defining what is kinship care. This study offers one definition – but there is an urgent need to move towards a definition which is shared by all the agencies, government departments and individuals with an interest in this issue.

- The needs of children and young people are paramount in deciding which is the most appropriate living arrangement when they can no longer live or return to live with their birth parent(s).

- Unlike fostering, adoption and residential care, kinship care does not have a dedicated organisational structure or focus; this is needed as a matter of priority for it to be a coherent placement option. There are a number of different ways that this could be done and an examination of different practice models, including case management, would be a good place to start.

- A service exclusively provided for kinship carers affording them the same priority as foster carers may better address partnership issues between carers and social workers.

- The group of young people in the study (average age 16.5 years) expressed needs for independent living, for housing, for financial support, training, education and employment advice. When considering a 'kinship care service', local authorities may need to consider the range of services needed for young people in transition rather than trying to accommodate quite different needs within a children's services structure.

- The kinship care placements that 'work best' according to the young people, the carers and the social workers, are those that are consensual, and in many cases these are initiated by the extended family. This raises questions about the limits of social services initiated kinship care placements.

1   Introducing kinship care

Policy background, research aims and methods

Definition of kinship care

The term 'kinship care,' is a difficult one to define in that it is used to describe different types of relationships, each carrying different legal responsibilities, obligations and consequences. Further there is very little research published about 'kinship care' in the UK to guide us in making a definition. It is of especial importance then that we produce a clear definition of the term 'kinship care', not only as an essential element of this study, but also because it has wider implications in terms of policy making and recommendations. According to McFadden (1998) writing in the USA, kinship care can be described as either an *informal* family arrangement, taking place outside the child welfare system, or a *formal* family arrangement, arranged and approved by child welfare agencies. This is a useful distinction to make and this study is concerned with the second of these arrangements, that is formal kinship care. Yet it should be noted that the existing US or UK literature does not make a further distinction within formal kinship care, since the relatives or friends may or may not be approved foster carers. The research study described here mostly concerns formal kinship care placements not subject to a fostering agreement.

In this study our working definition of a child living in a kinship care placement is as follows:

> A child living away from the parental home with a relative or friend and known to the social services department, and who would otherwise be with stranger foster carers, in residential care, independent living, or adopted. The kinship care placement is either initiated by the social services department or

via a relative or friend, and involves some sort of assistance or
arrangement, including making decisions about legal orders,
financial and social work support.

Although many of these children are likely to be subject to a court order, such as a
Residence Order, they are not required to be subject to a legal order for their carer
to receive financial or other support from social services. Falling within the terms of
the Children Act 1989 a Residence Order (a Section 8 Order) is 'a court order
stating with whom the child must live until they reach 16. The local authority loses
any parental responsibilities it held if the child was on a care order ...' (NFCA,
2000:11). In this study it is those kinship care placements which had been in
existence three months or more, whether or not they were on a Residence Order,
which fulfilled the research criteria of being in a kinship care placement or
arrangement. This minimum period was, in the absence of other guidance, drawn
from the eligibility criteria used in the Children Act 1989 and the Children (Leaving
Care) Act 2000. These state that children leaving care are entitled to services by
virtue of having been 'looked after' for that minimum period of three months.
While three months is a relatively short period of time, it was helpful in that it
excluded very temporary, short term kinship care placements involving staying away
from a birth parent with a relative or friend. It also avoided duplicating the previous
research findings conducted in the same borough, summarised below, about
ongoing and 'mature' that is, two years minimum kinship care placements.

Policy background

There are a number of important policy issues that bear on formal kinship care.
These centre on the increasing numbers of children in the public care system, and
the quality and lack of choice of other appropriate child welfare placements
available for a child or young person 'suffering or likely to suffer significant harm'
(The Children Act 1989).

Since 1994 the numbers of children being looked after have increased, with the
associated mix of benefits, risks and costs. There remain serious concerns about the
quality of care provided for these children in the looked after public care system. This
is especially so in relation to those in residential care (see, for example, Berridge,
1997) despite the continuing improvements brought about by the Department of
Health's Quality Protects Initiative (DoH, 1998b). Placement choice is restricted by
the shortfall in fostering resources especially for those in the teenage age groupings
i.e. the 13–16-years-olds. In 1998 half of all children starting to be looked after were

aged 10–17, and 14–16 years was the peak age group among the population of children being looked after. Recent studies (for example, Sinclair and others, 1995) have indicated that 10–17 year olds often receive little attention before admission and have identified a need for greater attention to preventive work with teenagers.

Since at least the mid-1980s governments have recognised that the outcomes for young people leaving care are poor and should be improved. For example, among many, the House of Commons Health Select Committee (DoH, 1998a) pointed to continuing, poor and unacceptable outcomes for young people leaving the care of local authorities. Improved services for care leavers remains a priority in the extended Quality Protects Initiative DoH (1998b). It is expected that the outcomes for care leavers will be improved as a result of the Children (Leaving Care) Act 2000. There is a lack of evidence about kinship care placements, either in terms of their numbers, the children and young people's views of living in such placements, or their durability.

There are also ongoing concerns about the disproportionate number of black young people in the looked after system, among young people leaving care, and in custodial and penal systems. The issue of achieving high quality appropriate services for black children and families, or 'cultural competence' is of especial relevance in kinship care.

In an attempt to estimate the scale of kinship care we added the figures for kinship care (fostering) estimated at 10 per cent nationally (Department of Health, 1999) together with the kinship care (non-fostering) figures, the focus of this research. The result was that kinship care provides an estimated 13–20 per cent of all social services placements in the London Borough of Wandsworth, where the research was conducted, and possibly elsewhere.

The policy relevance for kinship care also derives from legislation, in particular the Children Act 1989, which broadly supports kinship care. First, and in general terms, the Children Act 1989 imposed a new duty on local authorities 'to safeguard and promote the welfare of children in need' *(S.17)*. The term 'in need' is defined as those children unlikely to achieve or maintain, or have the opportunity of achieving or maintaining, a reasonable standard of health or development without the provision of services, and those children who are disabled *(S.17, para 10c)*. The main references for kinship care are (authors'emphasis):

- The Children Act 1989 *encourages placement* of that child *with a person connected with that child: a family member or relative, or 'other suitable person'* unless it 'would not be reasonably practicable or consistent with his welfare'. *(S.23, para 6)*

- In making decisions about a child to be looked after, the local authority must give *due consideration to the child's religious persuasion, racial origin, and cultural and linguistic background. (S.22, para 5c)*

- Before making any decision the local authority must ascertain, *as far as possible, the wishes of the child, his parents, anyone who holds parental responsibility, and anyone else* the local authority considers relevant. *(S.22, para 4a,b,c)*

- 'So far as is reasonably practicable and consistent' with the child's welfare, the accommodation *offered should be near the child's home and siblings should be accommodated together. (S.23, para 7)*

- A disabled child should have accommodation *not unsuitable for her/his needs. (S.23, para 8)*

- Formal kinship care is beginning to contribute to the Department of Health's Quality Protects placement stability policy agenda (Department of Health, 2000a; 2000c: 48; 2000d: 29) as it seeks to develop and explore other placement options for children in need.

The research study

Earlier research conducted at De Montfort University established the increasing use of kinship care within the Borough of Wandsworth and the high proportion of black children in kinship care (Laws and Broad, 2000; Broad, 2001b). However, that research had focused only on the views of kinship carers and social workers. Given the dearth of other research in this field, it was thought important to undertake more detailed research on the use of kinship care and, in particular, to capture the views of the young people themselves.

Aims of research project

The primary aim of this research was to examine the role and contribution of kinship care in supporting young people making the transition to adulthood. To achieve this we aimed to explore and record young peoples' and carers' experiences of formal kinship care. A major focus here was on the experiences and needs of black and minority ethnic young people and their carers. As a result of this research, it was hoped to draw out some implications for policy and practice.

The research also aimed to elicit the views of social workers on kinship care and their involvement in decision making, assessments and care plans. The views of social workers are inevitably critical in understanding the role, practice and limits of social services involvement in such placements.

The scope and limits of the study

The Joseph Rowntree Foundation funded this research under its 'Young People in Transition to Adulthood' programme. Accordingly, the research focused predominantly on the 14–21 age group. The task of the kinship carers with this age group was thought likely to be different from those caring for younger children, the main focus of the earlier research. Young people are more likely to want more independence and to challenge grandparents' wishes and views than younger children. Also, and critically, social services' legal responsibilities, structures and procedures do not readily apply to young people over 18.

Research sample and methodology

The research team systematically collected a wide range of information, gathered both from face-to-face interviews with young people, carers and social workers, and from general management information systems and individual social services files. Both young people and kinship carers were contacted first to seek their permission to participate, and second to gather information (anonymised) about them. A total sample of 50 young people were identified by Wandsworth Social Services as being currently in kinship care placements.

Selection of the sample

This research builds on an earlier smaller scale kinship care study conducted in the same authority (Laws and Broad, 2000). Eight young people aged over 14 years of age from that kinship care study were included in the present study plus other cases taken from the local social services children 'in need' database, with an added 'kinship care' field kindly produced for us by the social services department. Yet in the face of the small number of additional young people in kinship care aged over 14 recorded on that specially produced database (just 16 from a database of 73 children in kinship care), the details of further kinship care cases known at the team level and not yet recorded on the database were requested. This request took the form of a detailed memo sent to all the local authority's children and family social work teams. We also undertook two research and training presentations to inform social workers and managers about the study and stimulate interest in it. These actions eventually produced 26 additional cases. These multiple and time-consuming sampling and selection strategies were necessary to locate all the relevant kinship care placements. Eventually, after considerable work checking and tracking down cases and carers, the research team used this information to construct its own 'kinship care research database of young people 14 plus.' This consisted of a total sample of 50 cases.

Interviews

It was very difficult to find the contact details of many of these young people, especially the post 16–17 age group, who tended to move around between friends' accommodation, their carer's home and other places, including hostels for homeless young people, bed and breakfast accommodation and, in one case, custody. Telephone contact proved both advantageous and disadvantageous. Once the research team had obtained the telephone numbers of the carers, if these were known/available, these land line telephone links proved reliable for ongoing contact. Mobile phones, the preferred and costly choice of some of the young people, seem excellent for direct contact, providing the mobile phone was on, was working and was answered by the young person to whom it belonged. Where any one of these three conditions were not met, which was often, mobile phone contact became illusory and was more of a blight than a bonus.

It had already been decided that it might assist the young people's level of participation to provide a £50 voucher for each interview; vouchers from well known sports and clothes stores were especially popular and in one case a young man whose partner had given birth on the morning of the interview requested a voucher for a specialist baby and mother store. A system for dealing with ethical issues about participation was produced, which centred on establishing written and telephone contact, and 'contracts' with carers and young people about confidentiality and anonymity.

While the prime emphasis and aim of the project was to seek the views of the young people and carers, it was also important to seek the views of social services staff who have such an important part to play in terms of social work practice. The views of 25 social workers were obtained either through individual interviews or focus groups. These social workers were not necessarily involved in the kinship care placements in the research, nor were they necessarily involved with kinship care, but this provided a useful cross-section of children and families social workers' views about kinship care.

2 Characteristics of the young people, carers and placements

Introduction

This chapter describes the characteristics of the 50 young people, their kinship carers and details of their placements. Data had to be sought from a range of sources and in some cases neither the young person nor carer knew the detailed history of the placement; in others we did not consider it appropriate to ask them detailed factual questions. For these reasons, data was sometimes unavailable – even on important legal aspects of the current and prior placement.

1 Descriptive data about the young people in the study

Figure 2.1 Total sample of young people by age groupings

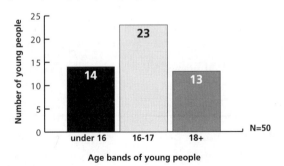

Age bands of young people

Age and gender

Forty-six, or 92 per cent, of the total number of young people in the sample were within the 14–25 year age range (four were aged 11–13) and the average age was 16.5 years. Approximately half the sample was in the 16–17 year old age band. There were more young women (30) than young men (20). Figure 2.1 shows the age groupings of the young people.

Ethnicity

The research team recorded the ethnic origin of the young people using the
Wandsworth Social Services Department race record-keeping categories and asked
young people and carers in interview, using those categories, to self-define their
ethnic ('racial/cultural') origin. Figure 2.2 displays the ethnic origin of the young
people.

Figure 2.2 Ethnicity of the young people

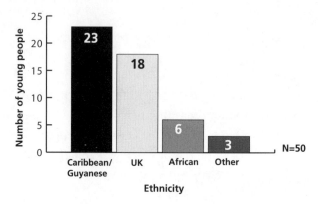

Note The three 'other' in this figure includes one of each of the following: 'other European' 'more than one of the above' and 'other'.

There are a total of 13 categories (including the above and also 'more than one of
these groups') listed on Wandsworth Social Service Department's race record-
keeping forms, as used by that local authority. These same categories were also used
for previous kinship care research conducted in that authority (Laws and Broad,
2000). For consistency therefore, the research team used those categories as the
basis for the young people self-defining their ethnic origin, rather than others, for
example 'Black British' or 'dual heritage'.

As can be seen from Figure 2.2, those young people in the 'Caribbean or Guyanese'
ethnic origin category formed the largest group, accounting for 23 (or 46 per cent)
of all responses (N=50), and the second largest group were those whose ethnic
origin was the 'UK' (English/Welsh/Scottish/Northern Irish) accounting for 18 (or
36 per cent).Those who were of African ethnic origin accounted for 6 (or 12 per
cent) of all responses. By comparison, only 16 per cent of all looked after children
in Wandsworth are Caribbean or Guyanese (London Borough of Wandsworth,
1997b). Here, therefore, the majority, 29 (or 58 per cent) of this kinship care
sample, were either of Caribbean or Guyanese or African ethnic origin. The finding
that a high proportion of children and young people in kinship care are from black

and minority ethnic families is also a finding in the American kinship care literature (McFadden, 1998; Ince, 2001), and in an earlier report (Broad, 2001b).

2 Descriptive data about the kinship carers in the study

Ethnicity

In all but one case, the ethnic origin of the young people was the same as that of the kinship carer. All kinship carers who responded indicated that English was their first language.

Age

Nineteen carers provided information about their age, and Figure 2.3 shows this information. Three kinship carers were aged 40 years or under, seven were aged between 40 and 60, and the biggest group, nine, were aged 61 and over (three of these were over 65). This is an older profile than that of foster carers who themselves are older than the general population of parents with dependent children (Triseliotis and others, 2000: 4). In one study it was found that 80 per cent of female foster carers were aged between 31 and 55 years (quoted in Hill, 1999: 79). Here a similar percentage, 74 per cent, were over 51 years of age. The age of these kinship carers alone would probably exclude their consideration as foster carers, even if they wished to be so assessed.

Figure 2.3 Kinship carers by age groupings

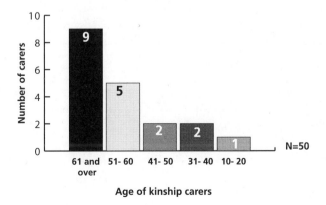

Note The ages of the remaining 31 kinship carers were not available/not provided.

Relationship to young person

Figure 2.4 Relationship of kinship carers to young people

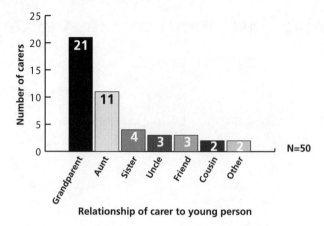

Relationship of carer to young person

Note Two responses (one young person with 'aunt and uncle' and one with 'step-father') are not shown in the figure. There were also two missing responses.

The three placements with friends were for young people over the age of 16 (17 and 18 year olds) and had been in existence for between one and three years. Therefore they are not 'private fostering' arrangements, and we do not know if they had previously been so.

Twenty-one (or 42 per cent) of all the kinship carers were grandparents (including only one grandfather), followed by 11 or 22 per cent who were aunts, and 4 or 8 per cent who were sisters (see figure 2.4). The majority, 34 (or 68 per cent) of the kinship carers were female (that is grandmother, sister, aunt and friend) emphasising and underscoring points about traditional caring responsibilities, roles and gender.

3 Descriptive data about the placement

Duration of current placement

Figure 2.5 Duration of current placements

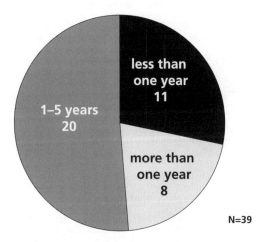

In interview carers were asked about the length of time the young person(s) had been living in the placement (this was also asked of the young person), and whether this period was continuous. The occasional night staying-over, for example with the young person's birth parent or at a friend's house, was still regarded as continuous living with the kinship carer. We also asked where the young person was living, for example in foster care or with birth parent(s), immediately prior to his or her current situation.

The research study found that of the 39 placements where details were available, 20 (or 51 per cent) had lasted continuously for between 1 and 5 years, 11 (or 28 per cent) for over 5 years, and 8 (or 21 per cent) for less than one year (Figure 2.5). The average length of the current placements was four years. In all but one case (a month-long placement) the placements ranged from three months to fifteen years two months in length. It is difficult to make comparisons with other forms of care (for example residential care or foster care) because the age profiles of Department of Health returns are predominantly for children up to 16 years of age. However, these 'duration of placement' figures do suggest a pattern of 'longer term stability' for the majority of the kinship care placements studied. In itself this is a significant finding. This was also the finding from the earlier study in Wandsworth (Laws and Broad, 2000).

Administrative categories

Other descriptive data recorded the different administrative categories used by social services and these are shown in Figure 2.6. The main significance of these 'administrative category' findings is their variation. Of all the 42 placements where the administrative category was known the biggest groupings were equally, those subject to Section 17 payments[1], and those 'not known' where the category was not known to the carer, social worker or young person. The next largest group, eight, consisted of those on a Residence Order, followed by seven on a Care Order. No further legal information is known about those on Care Orders. Section 17 is very broadly drawn and includes children with disabilities, neglected or abused children, children with developmental difficulties and children suffering social and emotional deprivation. It is the preferred funding source used by Wandsworth Social Services Department to support its various kinship care placements. The Borough makes Section 20[2] payments only for children in foster and residential care. Although the Borough actively promotes Residence Orders, only a comparatively low percentage (19 per cent) was recorded as being subject to a Residence Order. Residence Orders and Care Orders were made across the entire age range of the group whereas Section 17 was the legal basis on which support was provided for the older 16 – 19-year-olds.

Figure 2.6 Administrative categories of kinship care placements

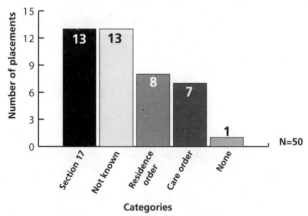

Note There were eight cases, not shown, where the information was 'missing', rather than provided, as 'not known' as presented in the figure.

---

1   Section 17 services are services provided under Section 17 of the Children Act 1989 to provide family support to children in need and their families.
2   Section 20 of the Children Act 1989 defines the local authority's duty to provide accommodation for under 16 and 16–18 year olds in need.

Previous administrative categories

The information that was gathered about previous placements indicated that 19 (or 38 per cent) of the 50 young people had previously been looked after. Of these, in two thirds of cases the young person had previously been looked after by another local authority and in a third, by Wandsworth Social Services. Twenty-four or 48 per cent had not previously been in the looked after system. In 16 of the latter cases the previous placement had been with their family, predominately their birth parent(s).

Routes into kinship care

The research showed that there are a number of different routes into kinship care.

1. A final resort for social services after other care options had failed.
2. A continuation of birth parent support to the young person's parent(s) already provided by the carer.
3. The first option for social services once the family situation had broken down.
4. An option selected by the young people themselves after a crisis at home.

Awkwardly these are not necessarily mutually exclusive routes. For example it is possible that a young person could have opted to live with an extended family member, and at the same time this was a first or final resort for social services. By far the majority of the placements identified in the report began after there was some sort of family breakdown.

Four of the carers took responsibility for the young person after other options had failed. One young man had spent about two years in residential care, but according to his carer was 'unhappy and unmanageable there'. A young woman had spent most of her early teenage years in residential care: her grandmother describes her time there as marked by frequent involvement with the police, absconding and drug abuse. A young woman had spent time in residential care and had moved to bed and breakfast accommodation, but was not managing to live independently. Another carer took responsibility once a foster care placement had broken down. Social services were involved in all placements.

In three cases, the grandparents were already involved, at least partially, in the care of grandchildren through supporting the birth parents who were having problems coping. The move to full time kinship care was a logical step when the birth parents could no longer manage to look after the young person. One grandparent explained: 'It didn't feel very different – I've always been looking after him. There was not much change for us.' Again social workers were involved in all these placements.

In only two cases were the carers the first port of call for social workers once it became clear that the young person could not live with the birth parents. In one instance the grandparents were initially asked to look after the young person for a period of respite, and this developed into more permanent care. In the other, a registered foster carer was asked to foster her half brother.

Two young people themselves selected kinship care. One grandmother for example explained how her 11-year-old grandson had a row with his mum who threw him out of her house: 'He rang me from a telephone box. I said, "Get into a cab now and come over straight to me". He's been here ever since' (seven years). Social services became involved through the local authority's Diversion Scheme. This scheme assists young people in need of advice and support outside children and families teams.

In another similar case, the carer's daughter was distressed about the fate of her 11-year-old friend who was drifting from living on the streets to living with young men, and asked whether her friend could move in. The carer approached social services as a last resort when it became clear she could no longer cope financially.

The young people's and carers' views on how their placement had come about are described respectively in chapters 3 and 4.

3 Young people's voices

The young people we interviewed presented us with a very wide range of experiences and personal stories. This chapter tells those stories. Some had been removed from their birth parents when babies and young children, and subsequently came to live with family or friends. Some had been asked to leave their family homes. Others had left of their own volition. A number of the older group were technically homeless, but were spending time with family or friends until other arrangements could be made. This chapter sets out their thoughts and feelings under the following main headings:

- how the young people came to be in kinship care
- the advantages of kinship care
- the limits of kinship care

Two case studies then follow which bring together many of the issues referred to in the preceding sections.

How the young people came to be in kinship care

For some young people kinship care was a natural extension, following a breakdown of one sort or another, to the family links that were already in place. Their earlier lives had often been chaotic and where there were partnership breakdowns, for example, the young person had tried living first with one parent and then the other, without success. These periods had been interspersed with time spent with grandparents, aunts and uncles, siblings and friends. Following particularly difficult crisis periods, involving for example parental illness (both physical and mental) there would be time spent in state care. These periods were characterised by young people remembering feeling vulnerable and unloved.

The research team had to be careful when talking to young people about how they came to be living with a kinship carer. We did not want to put them in a position where they felt they were 'betraying' a parent or where they had to divulge unwillingly their own troublesome behaviour. Some young people however, were happy to discuss the reasons why they were in kinship care, and three main reasons emerge. These of course are not mutually exclusive. Perhaps the most common reason was that the parent could no longer 'cope' mainly through ill health:

> 'Well, I was living with my Mum when I was little and my Mum got very ill so I had to come to live in London (with brothers and sisters). We kept going backwards and forwards to my Dad's house and sometimes they stayed at the weekends'.

> 'My Mum was very ill, so we've always stayed with her [grandmother] on and off, but I think I came for good in 1986'.

In some instances, ill health of the parent was combined with, or exacerbated by, the difficult behaviour of the young person:

> 'My Mum couldn't cope – I think her nerves are not as strong and she would have breakdowns and couldn't cope and stuff and so little minor things like getting into trouble at school or whatever she would go off the rails and couldn't really cope. Growing up now and moving out I've got a stronger bond – much better than living at home'.

Ill health also took the form of alcohol and drug dependency:

> 'Mum was an alcoholic and I just didn't get along with her, so I come, moved in with my Nan, and I've been here for two and a half years'.

> 'Basically troubles with my Dad, he had this girlfriend and started taking drugs and that, my sister looked after me'.

In a minority of cases, the young person recalled how their own chaotic lifestyles made it difficult for their birth parent.

> 'My Mum, my Dad, and me and the social workers had a part in it as well. But it was thought to be the best thing at the time, we tried everything when I was living with my Mum to make it better, but it wouldn't work. But then there was a time when I lived with my Mum, I got a handful, I was 14 … I went through a stage … where I got mugged in the street five times in six weeks

'… So, basically my Mum thought that with all the stress I was
going through and everything … My Dad was worried that they'd
take me in [in care], and it was best for me to move out really'.

The advantages of kinship care

- being 'rescued' from local authority care (residential/foster care)
- feeling safe
- maintaining links with family, siblings and friends
- feeling settled, being loved and cared for
- sustaining cultural/racial heritage
- supporting education/ambitions/achievements.

Being 'rescued' from local authority care

Most of the young people had spent time in local authority care and for most this
was a traumatic experience. They described frequent moves, feelings of rejection,
and an increasing sense of isolation. Two young people had been refused local
authority assistance since they did not want to reveal the exact nature of the
difficulties they were experiencing in their home lives.

Almost all those who had experience of local authority care described how desperate
they were to leave residential or foster care, or as one person put it: 'being
"rescued"', and another as 'being with people who you know and they know you'.
The young people we interviewed did not want to live with strangers. Some had
experience of family life and thought residential and foster care was a false
environment:

> 'I think foster carers should know what it feels like to be living
> with a total stranger, they just got paid for it, that's their job'
> *(male, aged 16, English/UK ethnic origin)*.

The older ones were especially frustrated because they were developing a mind of
their own, wanting more independence, and foster care ceased to become a relevant
option. As two young people said:

> 'I was staying around my friends' houses, staying outside with my
> friends, staying anywhere I could really, because I got kicked out
> of care' *(male, aged 16, English/UK)*.

'I've had a bad experience of foster care, I didn't want that'
(female, aged 18, Caribbean or Guyanese ethnic origin).

Feeling safe

Many young people spoke about needing to feel safe. For some, the behaviour of adults who they had previously been living with – birth parent(s), foster carer(s) or residential care workers – made them feel vulnerable and unsafe. They were exposed to both criminal activities and the effects of substance abuse. This was difficult for them to talk about and they felt that social services did not always believe them. They also felt pressurised to reveal home circumstances, which they often felt unable to do:

'I didn't really like it, my Mum wasn't really there all the time, she used to go out at night time and leave me there, I didn't like it at all. Many times I went to my next-door-neighbours crying, because I was scared. I didn't know where my Mum was, she didn't used to pick me up from school' *(male, aged 18, Caribbean or Guyanese).*

[talking about Mum] 'She's an alcoholic, she could do stupid things at the time, because before we had a fire and she got burnt bad, like the night we had the fire I got my little brother out' *(male, aged 16, English/UK).*

'I was having arguments with my foster parent, she was an alcoholic and we didn't know that, and she was not giving me the money she was supposed to give me, and she didn't like me standing up for myself, so she kicked me out, that was my last chance, because you can only stay in two, three, no two foster placements' *(male, aged 16, English/UK).*

'If I'd stayed there I would be in prison and other things' *(male, aged 17, Caribbean or Guyanese).*

Maintaining links with family, siblings and friends

This was important to most young people. They recognised the limits of not being able to live with their birth family, but wanted to maintain links, to know about them even if they could not live with them. Friends and people they had known in their earlier life were seen as important in feeling settled. The carers were seen as central to helping them maintain these links. There were, however, notable exceptions. Some young people felt they had been so 'let down' that they expressed a wish never to see certain family members again.

> 'I just wanted to be with people I knew and they knew me. Being with my brothers made it better and being with my Gran it made it better as well. I see both my Mum and Dad. My Mum comes round most weekends and my Dad he comes at the weekend as well' *(female, aged 15, Caribbean or Guyanese).*

> 'My sisters all live near to where my Mum and Dad live so I see them all the time' *(male, aged 15, learning difficulties, English/UK).*

> 'I had one friend especially, that I used to talk to (about her difficulties), she lived just down the road from me' *(female, aged 16, African).*

> 'Yeah, I know all the people around here' *(male, aged 16, Caribbean or Guyanese).*

Forty-one of the 46 young people indicated they had siblings (between one and seven). Many of the young people described the importance of keeping in touch with their brothers and/or sisters, although, surprisingly perhaps, 'maintaining contact with siblings' did not emerge as a finding in all cases. Siblings tended to be either still living with the birth parent, living with the young person in kinship care, or looked after. The majority of siblings were living with their birth parent(s) and this raises the question of why the young person interviewed, and not their brother or sister, was currently living in kinship care. There may be practical issues (that is, space in the house/rooms available) or other family, or child protection issues. One young person volunteered that her mother had never liked her and she had known this from a very early age:

> 'My Mum didn't like me, she was always swearing and shouting at me' *(female, aged 16, Caribbean or Guyanese).*

In discussing family relationships it often emerged that there were regular and ongoing family and sibling separations, but in a number of cases a brother and sister were brought up separately for long periods of time, sometimes in another town or even another country. Two young people spoke of their unhappiness in not being able to make contact with siblings for whom the family links have been lost and these may be siblings who have subsequently been adopted.

Feeling settled, being loved and cared for

Many of the young people spoke of feeling loved by the people they were now living with. These were not necessarily biological families, but were the people who cared for them and they chose to call their family. There was also a sense of needing to be settled to take stock of what had happened in the light of earlier upheavals. For example:

> 'My Gran, she's 100 per cent, she's been our rock and kept the whole family together. If it wasn't for her we would probably all be separated and not grown up with each other and not as close as we are. I wouldn't be the stable person I am today if it wasn't for my Gran' *(female, aged 25, English/UK).*

> [living with grandma] 'I actually like it here, because if I didn't come here I wouldn't have met the people I'd met, I reckon I wouldn't be as advanced as I am now, 'cause I think staying with my Mum I'd have been kind of held back in certain things. I look at my brother and sister [still living with Mum] and I think I could have been like that at the age of 10. But I wouldn't have liked to have been like that. I'd rather be the way I am now. It wouldn't have done me a whole lot of good' *(male, aged 18, Caribbean or Guyanese).*

> 'I've had a happy life with my Nan' *(male, aged 16, English/UK).*

There was a striking amount of maturity and emotional literacy expressed in a very open manner by three young people:

> [talking about his step-father] 'Moving back with my Dad is one of the things that I am very proud of because through all the time I was in care that's what I wanted to do. My Dad made regular visits to me once a week, took me out to the cinema, other things, and basically everything I wanted to do. I wanted to live with my Dad' *(male, aged 17, English/UK).*

> 'I think it makes you more secure that you are living with someone who loves you' *(male, aged 19, Caribbean or Guyanese).*

> 'I love to know that I belong to somebody, I'm loved by people and it's good to know that I've got somewhere to come after school that I can call home' *(female, aged 15, English/UK).*

As well as having their emotional needs met, young people described how their physical needs were met which resulted in a feeling that they were nurtured and cared for. This was valued and was seen in direct contrast to their earlier experiences of often being left to fend for themselves:

> 'I relied on Nan and Grandad for my feelings and I would cry and my Nan and Grandad could talk to me and help me through it' *(female, aged 18, English/UK)*.

> [on coming to stay with grandmother] 'I hadn't had a wash for how long? My clothes were disgusting and I was very skinny, very under-weight, that's about it. It was bad, very bad' *(male, aged 17, Caribbean or Guyanese)*.

> 'I've known that I've got a dinner here if I need it, at my Mum's sometimes we wouldn't get a dinner, or we would, she'd buy us a takeaway, but it ain't the same as like knowing that dinner's there on the table' *(male, aged 16, Caribbean or Guyanese)*.

Racial and cultural heritage

As stated earlier, 58 per cent of the young people in the study were of Caribbean, Guyanese or African ethnic origin. We were particularly interested to understand their experiences and wondered if their background played any part in their choice to live with grandparents, siblings and extended relatives. The young people themselves largely made the choice, but there were clear benefits to them in the development of their identity. As one young person said:

> 'You have your own culture, so I think it's important to live with someone who knows about your cultural background, you don't have to, but I think it's better' *(female aged 16, Caribbean or Guyanese)*.

Step-relations were generally just part of the 'family'. Three young people described their situation as follows:

> 'My step-Dad, he's black, my step Gran's black, that's just how my family is, if I'm happy with it, so if anyone else has got a problem with it that's up to them. I'm part of the family, so they all call me grandchild and sister, so I just feel part of the family now' *(female, aged 15, English/UK)*.

> 'I don't feel that I've been brought up as a black British person;
> I've been brought up as a normal person' *(male, aged 18,
> Caribbean or Guyanese)*.

> 'Cause I'm half black and half white, there's all different shades
> of black isn't there, there's dark black, light black and there's
> black people who are my colour. I just see myself as myself'
> *(female, 21, English/UK)*.

We asked if there had been any experience of racist behaviour towards them. Some young people did say they remember feeling this when they were in primary school, but they also spoke of bullying. One white young woman explained that she experienced problems in maintaining a relationship with her black boyfriend. This came from her biological parents, not from her grandmother, with whom she was living. Most young people had friends from different ethnic groups, some of whom were of very long standing. Overall, the response to racist behaviour was one of 'well you've got to deal with it, haven't you'.

Education, achievements and ambitions

We were especially keen to find out how the young people were coping with schools, colleges and their first jobs, as this would be an important indicator of how kinship care is helping them making the transition into adulthood. This is especially relevant since all the young people in this group have experienced disruption in their lives and education has frequently been a casualty of that disruption, or, as one person put it:

> 'When Nan would send us, or take us to school, it was the first
> time we actually went to school, so it was like being thrown into
> hot water' *(female, 25, English/UK)*.

The support they have received (or not) has been critical in their ability to re-establish their education and to progress towards the realisation of their ambitions.

The research revealed some real success in re-establishing education patterns. All the young people recognised the importance of education, and one young person was taking 10 GCSEs. Most were seeking to attend further education and were keen to get qualifications. Some recognised that they were capable of better results and wanted to improve their skills. All the interviewees appeared to have a clear idea of the type of employment they would like:

'I didn't really take it seriously enough, I thought it would be easy. I didn't really get really good results, but I got enough to get to college' *(male, aged 18, Caribbean or Guyanese)*.

[previously suspended] 'I went to college last year and I did a GNVQ in IT, computers and I joined a computing training agency in …, and they set you up for interviews in offices and on the first interview I got the job – so I'm working. I'm on work-based training so when I've finished I'm on Level 2, move to Level 3, pass level 3 and I get an A Level in IT' *(male, aged 17, English/UK)* .

[currently suspended] 'I definitely want to go back and get an education. I really enjoy school and I have always been a regular attender. I want to get my GCSEs and I know I can do really well. I want to be a lawyer' *(female, aged 16, Caribbean or Guyanese)*.

In asking the young people to talk to us about what they considered to be their 'best achievement', it was hoped to get some measure of their self-esteem. Only one young person failed to name anything:

'I don't feel proud of nothing' *(female, aged 16, Caribbean or Guyanese)*.

Some spoke of now being able to help and support those who had cared for them. Others described things they had achieved with regard to leisure activities and attainments at college (having failed to make progress in the school environment). The wide range of achievements is summed up in the following quotations from some of the young people:

'… finishing my Level 1 NVQ 'cos I thought I wouldn't have passed it 'cos my reading and stuff like that' *(male, aged 17, English/UK)*.

'I'm caring full-time for my Mum now' *(male, aged 21, English/UK)*.

'Living until I was 16 – I thought I was going mad' *(male, aged 18, English/UK)*.

'Leaving the kids' homes' *(female, aged 18, English/UK)*.

As well as discussing the advantages of living in kinship care, the young people also pointed out its limitations.

The limits of kinship care

- limitations to freedom
- financial hardship
- transition to independence.

We found that where the young people had settled and the arrangement was long standing, there they were more likely to understand the sacrifices made by their carers. To this extent they were reluctant to talk about any difficulties they may have been having at home. But problems were raised, and these are discussed below. Those living with grandparents, particularly lone grandparents, felt a responsibility to help out.

Limitations on freedom

Many young people are frustrated about their lack of independence, and those living in kinship care are no exception. The following comments are typical of many teenagers living at home: wanting to have friends around, play music, choose clothes, go out and live a modern lifestyle.

> 'I don't get any independence myself, my Nan moans sometimes about my things, my music when it's – well, there's loud and loud, and what I play isn't loud.' *(male, aged 17, Caribbean or Guyanese).*

> 'Nan is an older class person so she says it's not right for boys to go round touching girls and that. So if I have a girlfriend, then I have to go out' *(male, aged 16, English/UK).*

Sometimes the problems were compounded by lack of space. For example one young person was living with grandparents in single bedroom accommodation.

> 'I ain't got my own bedroom, and not being able to have my friends in like, in my own bedroom' *(male, aged 16, English/UK).*

Financial hardship

We found that there was a big issue about discretionary payments paid by the local authority. This was often compared with the amounts of money paid to foster carers, especially as siblings were often in foster care placements. The young people spoke of brothers or sisters getting better clothes and more opportunities because they were accommodated by the local authority. This was especially hard since many of the grandparents concerned were in receipt of basic state pensions only. According to three young people:

> 'Nan can't afford nothing, it's a struggle' *(male, aged 17, Caribbean or Guyanese).*

> [talking about his brother in foster care] 'Yeah, he quite likes it, he's got a jacuzzi in his house – doing better than us' *(male, aged 16, English/UK).*

> [talking about money] 'I was getting nothing from the college, so that's why I quit 'cause Nan was nagging at me, that's why I got to go to work' *(male, aged 16, English/UK).*

Transition to independence

For those who had been helped by an independent living scheme, there was positive feedback. However it was only available to those young people who have been accommodated by the local authority and was not available for those young people who were currently living in kinship care and not subject to a legal order. This was often despite the fact that they had previously been accommodated by the local authority, but had been unable to remain contained in local authority care. Because of this anomaly those young people wanting to make the transition from kinship care were in a particularly difficult situation. As three young people said:

> 'They asked me questions about living here and getting a flat, and asked if I'd like to when I'm 18 and then you hear nothing about it from them' *(male, aged 17, Caribbean or Guyanese).*

> 'Well he was talking about getting a hostel, staying in a hostel and then hopefully I'd get a flat out of it, or a room. I don't really want to go into a hostel' *(male, aged 16, English/UK).*

> 'I do want a flat because my Dad said when I'm 18, he wants me out anyway and like my Nan and Grandad are getting older' *(female, aged 17, English/UK).*

Case studies

The two case studies that follow bring together many of the issues discussed so far in this chapter. The names of the young people in these case studies have been changed.

Case study 1: 'Lateesha' (aged 16, Caribbean or Guyanese ethnic origin)

Lateesha came to live with her aunt when she was 14 years old. She had been in foster care where 'nothing really worked out'. She was in contact with her grandparents but felt her maternal grandmother was taking her mother's side. Her reason for leaving home was that her mother 'didn't like me, she was always swearing and shouting at me'. Lateesha explained that she knew she was being treated differently from her siblings from an early age, 'I knew she didn't want me'. Lateesha has three sisters and twin brothers. Her brothers now live with their father and two sisters live with their mother. She does not want to live with her mother or father. She expressed sadness at 'having been pushed out'.

Lateesha has been involved with three or four social workers. She spoke with sadness about how some had left once she had got to know them. She felt that there had not been time to get to the issues about her life. She said of her current social worker, 'he's more like a mate, I hope he will be my social worker, until I get sorted out'.

Lateesha is currently excluded from college: 'I have been excluded several times, sometimes for fighting, I get into trouble'. Lateesha explained that she had enjoyed school, always attended well and knew that she could do really well. Her ambition is to be a lawyer. Her social worker describes her as a bright, popular girl with many friends. Her time is spent mostly with her sister and her cousins. They spend time together, watch TV and about once a month go to the cinema. She explained that she was too short of money to do anything else. Lateesha wanted most 'to be independent as soon as I can'.

Case study 2: 'Jerome' (aged 18, Caribbean or Guyanese ethnic origin)

Jerome came to live with his grandparents just before he was five years old. He has three brothers and one sister, 'one of my brothers is with my mum, another is with another family, another is with another family and my sister is with my Mum as well'. Jerome's grandfather told us that he had taken to Jerome when he first saw him as a newborn in hospital. His mother could not cope with him.

Jerome described his early life at home as being one of fear. He was left alone at night and was often to be found knocking on the doors of neighbours for help. He was not picked up from school and suffered anxiety and uncertainty. Jerome remembered the early days with his grandparents and said that he was difficult to handle and had given them a hard time. He has been very happy living with his grandparents and had no plans to move on. He said he had benefited from the attention he had received and the guidance and support he experienced. Jerome has finished his GCSEs and is attending college studying electrical engineering. He is planning to take further courses in IT.

Jerome enjoys a good social life with his mates. He described his primary school days as him being pretty much an angry kid 'because of my moving from my mum at such an early stage, and not knowing why. I was always angry, I was the school bully that everyone was afraid of, but as I got older I changed, I transformed'. Coming to stay with his grandparents was a big change for Jerome, 'I had like family around me, I'd never experienced anything like that'. Jerome appreciates that his grandparents talk to him about life and their experiences and this has helped him to prepare himself. Jerome had visited his extended family in Jamaica. This was paid for by the local authority. He described his visit as 'just hot and that's how I thought of it, it was hot and I got a few sweets, met a few people'. He sees his life in this country.

Jerome expresses himself as happy with the life he has had with his grandparents. He has noticed that his brothers in foster care, and the siblings with his Mum, have not done so well in life. He considers himself very lucky to have been with his grandparents.

4 Kinship carers' views

This chapter presents the carers' perspectives of kinship care. It starts by looking at the reasons for the carers' involvement in the placement and then moves on to describe how kinship care affects the day-to-day lives of the young people and carers. Finally, the chapter examines carers' views of the impact of kinship care on the young person, the carers themselves and the wider family. The carers' support needs are discussed in the following chapter.

Reasons for carers' involvement with kinship care

Almost without exception the carers spoke passionately in favour of kinship care and gave the following reasons for their involvement:

- their love for the young person and (in the case of grandparents) love for and the desire to support the birth parent(s)
- a belief that family is the best place for children, and
- a distaste for the alternative – local authority care
- it better enables the young person to maintain links with birth parents
- it promotes or maintains a young person's racial, religious and cultural heritage.

These reasons closely match those given by the young people themselves in chapter 3.

Love

The carers described their love for these young people: 'I just love him to bits' was a typical statement. Some grandparents described with pride how they were present at the birth, and many had looked after their grandchildren for short periods at least from a very early age. An associated emotion was the desire to protect the grandchildren, especially if the carer believed that they have suffered enough already.

> 'To have your own mum saying "I don't want you" is bad enough,
> but to have your gran say that too …'

Equally, the grandparents loved and were concerned for their own children – the birth parents. Looking after their children's children was therefore a way of demonstrating that love: 'I could help my daughter to help herself'. The longer-term aim of some carers was to re-unite the young person with their birth parents.

The family model

Without exception, carers believed that the family is the best place in which to raise children:

> 'They are with family who know them better than anyone else –
> you might get a few hiccups with them, but life is full of hiccups'.

> 'I did not want my grandchildren to grow up in a different
> environment and with different people from their family'.

> '[grandparents] know more about the children and their
> backgrounds. Other people wouldn't know how they feel unless
> they have gone through it with them. You know the children
> inside out. You know their likes and dislikes, their little habits,
> what they can do and what they can't do …'

> 'No grandchild of mine will be put into care'.

The concept of 'family' was equally strong in cases where a friend is caring for the young person. Here the carer described how she has created a new family for the young woman concerned:

> 'She'll always have a family. She'll always have a Mum and sisters.
> Her children will have grandparents, aunties and uncles and
> cousins'.

Being raised by the family, maintaining links with birth parents and their cultural heritage are ways in which the young person's identity are defined and formed.

Maintaining links with birth parents

Four carers mentioned that they could provide a means whereby links with the birth parents and any siblings could be better maintained, or as one carer put it: 'She and her mum are close'. One set of grandparents is sharing the care of the young person with the birth parents, where the granddaughter goes each weekend. Other grandparents have moved to the same small estate as their daughter so that the grandson can have daily contact with his mother.

Maintaining racial and cultural heritage

We specifically asked carers about how they assessed the importance of young people maintaining their racial, cultural and religious identities as they grow up, and were in many cases surprised by the strength of feeling these questions provoked. A minority of carers described how important the family's ethnic heritage was to the young person:

> 'She loves listening to her great grandmother who talks in brogue. She likes to know her family history'.

Another carer described the value of social services paying her grandson's airfare to Jamaica so that he could meet many of his relatives for the first time. Other carers, both black and white, argued that the quality of love and care they provided were much more critical than race and ethnicity, for example:

> 'It doesn't matter what religion or culture you belong to – it's more important that a child is loved, fed and looked after',

or that the racial complexity of their own families made the question irrelevant:

> 'I'm from Yorkshire, his granddad was from Nigeria. Everything today is such a melting pot. These things don't make any difference to them [young people]' *(grandparent)*.

Perhaps surprisingly religion was a less sensitive subject for both the carers and researchers. Just under half the carers spoke of the importance of their faith and how at once stage they encouraged the young people to participate. Only one young person however remained actively involved in religious practice – the granddaughter of a practising Baptist who has become a Muslim. Elsewhere, carers accepted, in some cases sadly, that any religious affiliation must be the decision of a young adult:

> 'You can't force children who don't want to come. It's got to be their choice'.

Distaste for local authority care

Most carers expressed their aversion to local authority care, which was for most of the young people the only alternative. This distaste was partly a result of the stigma attached to such provision, partly the fear of strangers taking control of the young people, but mostly a belief that local authority care simply does not work, as the following quotes from grandparents illustrate.

> 'We did not want them to be brought up in a home. You hear about things there and read about them in the papers'.

> 'He would have kept changing and changing home. This mucks about their lives. Their whole life changes because of it'.

According to the carers all but one described the decision to take in the young person into their care was theirs and theirs alone, or as one carer put it, 'We needn't have looked after him – we just wanted to'. Another said 'There was no pressure. No one was forcing us. We were always told "It is up to you"'. Of course, it could be very difficult for someone to admit that she or he was reluctant to take on the care of a young relative or friend, but the research team considered that only two people had significant reservations. One explained: 'No, I didn't have the choice, but I was happy thinking that it would be for a few months, not for as long as it has been … I could well do without it really'.

Having established the reasons why the young people were living in kinship care we shall now consider what it is like living in kinship care.

Living in kinship care

This section describes any lifestyle changes the young person had to make after they had moved in – whether for example the carer expected different standards of behaviour or whether they had different attitudes towards clothes, meal times, music and so on.

> 'I treat him [the young person] as I treated my own [children]'.

> 'She is a normal 15-year-old girl. I have to know where she is going. We will take her and collect her. I did that with my own children'.

This approach worked well in the cases of the carers quoted above, or called for only minor or occasional adjustments. In another case one young man's girlfriend came to stay after she had a row with her parents. When the carer discovered that she was aged under 16- years-old he was concerned and restricted the number of friends who could stay. In another case a grandmother described how she has to continually remind her grandson to turn down the music as it is unfair to other people in the block, but she put this down to 'normal teenage stuff'.

However, some of the above carers described how dramatic changes in behaviour had to be called for when the young person moved in with the carer. In one instance a young woman had previously been living, at various times, either on the street or with older men and had a long history of being abused. Her carer explained:

> 'I had to "retrain" her. I had to teach basic things like how to wash, personal hygiene, eat with a family ... little things like put dirty clothes in the wash bag. She always used to eat as if it were going to be her last meal ... It was like starting all over again with a three-year-old ... She didn't know the basic things that a mum teaches you. She had reached puberty ... she didn't know about women's things, about what to do with periods ... Her sexual behaviour was very strange ... attention seeking ... craving for male attention. She would bring men back here, give out her phone number to strangers ... I had to teach her how to be safe'.

Another carer described the problems she had with her granddaughter who had come to stay with her after leaving residential care:

> 'I had to wean her off drugs and change the way she dressed. I never allowed her to go out showing her backside off'.

The granddaughter referred to in this quote wanted to visit her old friends from residential care. The carer felt these friends would be a bad influence. She prevented this by putting the granddaughter into debt by lending her money for cigarettes so that she could not afford the fare.

Around half the carers described how difficult it was to agree standards of behaviour with the young people they were looking after. In some cases it was possible to see how the usual teenage tussles are compounded by the additional generation gap brought about by grandparenting:

> 'He doesn't like what [clothes] I have bought. He only wants things with labels. I want him to buy a suit, but he's not

interested. I told him to buy proper shoes. He will only wear trainers – but I suppose that is because other boys do. I gave him some money to buy a winter coat, but he came back with a light one … He should have more respect for the both of us. He doesn't do what he is told all the time … He has secrets – especially where girlfriends are concerned'.

Another grandparent described how the grandson she was looking after had very difficult behaviour and was frequently suspended from school:

'I have tried to establish boundaries with him. I say that if he behaves he can go out. But [name of grandson] turns round and says that if he can't go out he won't go to school at all. He waits until I am in a certain room where I can't see him and then sneaks out … He gets me so wound up'.

A further grandparent was also finding her grandson's behaviour difficult to manage:

'I would like him to have regular work or go to college … He went on a youth training course but left as he didn't like it … He expects me to keep him. ... He has given me about £60 since June [eight months ago]. He says, "My mates don't have to give their mums anything" … I tried to impose rules – to be in at a certain time, to clean the bath out after he had used it. It was no big deal but he didn't like them very much'.

The carer quoted here also believed her grandson had a gambling problem. She had accidentally come across his bank book and found that all his wages from a temporary job had disappeared:

'I gave him money to go to work and packed his lunches – but all he did with his wages was spend it on the machines'.

Impact of kinship care on the young person

This section looks at the carers' overall assessment of how well the placement was working; what they were especially pleased with and whether there had been any disappointments; and what they think would have happened to the young person if kinship care were not an option.

The positive aspects

Almost all carers believed that the overall impact of the placement has been positive and they identified a number of positive aspects in relation to:

- establishing a family life and security for the young person
- improved behaviour of the young person
- educational achievements
- maintaining links with the birth family.

In relation to establishing a family life and improved behaviour the following comments were typical:

> 'I've seen real changes in [name of young person's] behaviour. She is part of the family. She has become secure'.

> 'He has the family life with me and my son that he never had at home. He has been able to become an ordinary teenager'.

> 'Everything has worked out well … I'm very proud of him. He's very sensible. He's very clean and tidy. When he's out, he always rings to see how I am. He always lets me know where he is. He's not one for gallivanting off.'

Almost all carers mentioned educational improvements of which they are especially proud:

> 'He's done well at school – he's going to college. He'll be all right. I'm not worried about him. He's got his head screwed on …'

> 'I got her back into school. She missed two years of education – she had a poor school record … Now she's taking five GCSEs'.

> '[Name of young person] is doing very well at school – she is getting top marks and is planning a career in the caring for children'.

Some carers were especially pleased by the way in which the young person has been able to re-establish or maintain links with the birth parents. One grandparent reported: 'she has renewed her relationship with her mum', and 'they are not having the rows they used to have'. Another grandparent is sharing the care of the young person with the birth parents; the granddaughter stays with her grandmother each weekend. In another case, the grandparents have managed to organise a council exchange so that they are living on the same small estate as their daughter – this means the grandson has daily contact with his mother.

In a few cases, however the outcomes were seen as much more of an absence of the negative, for instance:

> 'I'm pleased they are not tearaways. I've been able to keep them out of trouble'.

> 'He hasn't run away. He hasn't been involved with the police'.

Some disappointments

A minority identified disappointments in terms of the young person's behaviour. Two seemed totally unhappy with the whole experience. They both described how difficult it was to manage their grandson's behaviour; one of the young people was moved to a special education school, but the other still lived with his grandmother. She reported:

> 'It's affecting my life and I don't think he's getting anywhere with his'.

A third carer felt her grandson has underachieved in his education:

> 'I'm not very pleased. I think he should have done better at school … But I think I should have got more help in this'.

What would have happened otherwise?

Carers were asked what they believe would have happened to the young person if they had not been able to look after him or her.

Almost all felt the only alternative was local authority care and viewed this as a disaster. In some cases this was because the young person had special needs and would have struggled with what carers saw as a more impersonal environment:

> 'It would have been a disaster if he had gone into a home. He's always had love around him. He wouldn't have coped … Going into care would have hurt him … he is quite timid'.

Others concurred with the view that the young person would not have thrived without the love offered within the family and which simply could not be found in any other environment.

'I have a feeling that foster carers would not sit down and talk to the children in the same way as a grandmother. It is not because they wouldn't have the time, but they may just be embarrassed talking like that … I know that grandparents have a different feeling for grandchildren [from foster carers]. I feel I care more for my grandchildren and in a different way than others would. I love my grandchildren regardless'.

Another carer, who had first-hand experience of local authority care, believed that the young person she was looking after would:

'…have become just another forgotten kid in care abandoned when she was 16…. She would have ended up pregnant'.

One carer however did wonder whether residential care could help her grandson to become less self-centred:

'Maybe it would have done [name of young person] good to have gone into care. Maybe when he wants new trainers and feels sorry for himself, then he would understand that life can be difficult'.

Impact on the carer

The carers also described how their lives have changed as a result of looking after the young people.

The benefits of being a carer

All carers reported at least one of the following positive aspects of looking after the young people:

- they provide companionship
- satisfaction in watching the person develop
- new interests.

Some young people were providing support and companionship for their carer. One, for example, was beginning to take over the care of his grandmother who was losing her eyesight and who described their relationship as: 'We're a couple of mates'. Another grandmother described how her granddaughter supported her and her husband through times of sickness. A third explained how she had spent all her adult life rearing children:

> 'I would be lonely without young people in my life. I wouldn't want to be alone now'.

Others described the benefits more in terms of the satisfaction they received through helping the young person:

> 'It's nice to think I can do things for [young person]. I'm trying to help him have a normal life'.

Another carer described the joy she felt watching the young person develop:

> 'I get some benefits. I can see a real change in her. She is intelligent and articulate. My main interest is helping her to have proper relationships with people – she is a person in her own right … I feel like my family has expanded – now I've got an even bigger family'.

In some cases however this was perhaps more of a remembered pleasure relating to when they were young children, rather than a current one. For instance, one grandmother described how:

> 'I used to take them here and there – all sorts of different places. Every year we went to the seaside. The best of it was the energy I received',

and how her husband:

> 'Loved it when the boys were here. He always used to ask, "Can the boys watch football with me tonight?" I said, "Yes, as long as he got them up in the morning". He was very happy'.

Carers also described how they are developing new interests and outlooks. For example:

> 'It's provided a new dimension as we've got older. He wanted to join the TA, so we went along to see them. We had to learn how to sort out a new school for him. He has his friends around …'.

The drawbacks of being a carer

Almost all carers described drawbacks, the main ones being:

- shortage of money
- loss of freedom and independence

- overcrowding
- age and ill health
- managing difficult behaviour.

Shortage of money

The financial burden of kinship care was predicted from our experience in earlier studies. The problem is hardly surprising given that the majority of carers are grandparents living on a pension, having no capacity to increase their incomes and, unlike prospective parents, no time to plan for the additional responsibilities. The following comments were typical:

> 'I haven't any money to buy my own clothes. I have to borrow from my daughter'.

> 'By the time I have finished paying, I don't have a ha'penny for myself ... I've never had a holiday since 1992'.

> 'Money is always a problem ... when a teenage girl goes out shopping they have to get all these accessories for their fingers and hair'.

Carers also worried about how financial hardship was affecting the young people themselves. They spoke for example of how siblings in foster or residential care fared much better materially than the young people they were looking after.

> 'It upset me to see what the girls were getting ... clothes allowance, pocket money, holidays. They went all over the world – America you name it, and all through that time poor [name of young person] never even got as far as Brighton ... All his clothes were passed down to him from his older cousin. But he never said anything when they [his sisters] were showing off their new clothes'.

Loss of freedom

We didn't predict the strength of feeling associated with the loss of freedom and independence – this was mentioned by almost three-quarters of the carers in the sample. Although the numbers involved are small it is perhaps worth noting that the lone carers felt this problem most acutely. In some cases the loss of freedom was associated with the everyday demands of looking after the young person:

> 'I can't go out anywhere. I have to be back to let him in and cook
> him a meal'.

But more often, carers feared the consequences of leaving the young person alone at home, usually because their behaviour was difficult:

> 'Other people my age have so much freedom. If I go out, I always
> have to think about what the boys are up to …'

> 'When your child is 16 you think you can start to have some life
> of your own, but I can't go out anymore – I can't leave her on
> her own. She has to be supervised.'

> 'It has stopped me from going out. I used to spend weekends
> with my mates in Bromley. I used to go on holidays, do Karaoke
> … I don't want to leave him … I don't know what they [the
> grandson and his friends] would do here if I'm away'.

An associated problem was the carers' social isolation: none of their peers were in a similar position. This was especially true for grandparents and single carers. One such carer described how she had lost touch with a lot of her friends, and although she has met some local mums, they were, inevitably, much younger. Forming new relationships was also more difficult for this carer. She had discovered that men her age were wary of her caring responsibilities. Another carer said that the placement was possible only because she was now single:

> 'If I had a partner, I wouldn't have been able to take him [her
> grandson] on'.

Overcrowding

Another major problem was overcrowding or lack of space. On reflection perhaps, this is not surprising as people rarely plan for kinship care, and this was certainly true of the three carers who described the problem. One carer, for example, lived in a one-bedroom flat. At one stage she was looking after two grandsons and their father who were all sleeping in her small sitting room. Another carer described how lack of suitable accommodation, a two-bedroom flat in the north of the borough, prevented her from looking after all three of her grandchildren – two girls and a boy. She therefore tried to look after the girls in a son's home in the south of the borough. Each afternoon she would catch a bus to the south of the borough and pick the girls up from school, all three would return by bus back to the flat in the north where the grandmother would feed the three grandchildren and the grandfather. After the meal she and the girls would catch the bus back to the home in the south of the borough where they would sleep. In the morning she would return home. The grandmother, then aged 72, managed this arrangement for five months, before it proved too much for her. The girls then went into foster care.

Age and ill-health

Some carers who were grandparents identified additional advantages relating to their age, experience and retirement status:

> 'We are both here all the time. When we had our children we were both at work. When [name of young person] comes home from school we are both here to talk to him. We also have a lot more patience than we had with our own children'.

> 'When you get older, you can see things more clearly, you have more patience and more time'.

However a more common response was an underestimate of the demands made by looking after young people:

> 'When I first took them in I thought, "This will be a doddle. I've bought up five children on my own"'.

Some grandparents found the combination of increasing age, declining health and demanding teenagers difficult:

> 'He expects me to play football with him at weekends. I do my best, but I get knackered'.

A second grandparent described how she had recently been diagnosed with diabetes and her poor health was restricting joint activities with her granddaughter; a third is losing her eyesight which is limiting her ability to look after her grandson. Another spoke of high blood pressure, resulting in part from the stress of looking after two grandchildren as well as helping her daughter to stay 'in rehab' to deal with her drug problems.

Even younger carers were having difficulties because of ill health. One has been looking after a daughter's friend for nearly four years and has recently started to look after the brother. She has two daughters of her own at home. This carer has MS and predicts that she will become wheelchair dependent within a year.

Managing difficult behaviour

As we have seen in this study, some young people have difficult behavioural problems and have been damaged by earlier life experiences. Carers referred to such behaviour as a drawback. Some carers found their status ill-defined and ambiguous, especially in terms of imposing discipline:

> 'With your children you can enforce boundaries because you are their mother. They have come from your body. But you can only go so far with them if you are their grandmother. You are not really their parent.'

Impact on the wider family

We wanted to know whether taking on caring responsibilities affected carers' relationships with other members of the family, including, where relevant, partners, other children and grandchildren. At the time of the research five of the 13 carers interviewed were living with a partner or spouse, and the partner of an additional carer was in prison. Without exception, the carers described how they shared the responsibility with their partners and the continuing support they received from them. No one mentioned any harmful effects on their relationships.

A more complex picture emerged when wider family relationships were discussed. In around half the cases, carers reported that these remain strong, for example:

> 'Everyone is really pleased because [young person] has turned out so well ... all the cousins are as thick as thieves'.

> 'My husband's mum is happy ... she had even more grandchildren. My daughters feel that they have a new sister ... it's just an expansion of the family'.

Elsewhere, carers described how family members were concerned about, and quite often resented, the additional responsibilities, and how existing relationships were disrupted. One grandmother remembered:

> 'My children told me I was a mug. They said, "You'll be sorry"'.

Another described how her youngest son was living with her at the time her two grandsons moved in.

> 'He was very jealous at first ... He didn't realise that they were just children and was constantly having a go at [young person]'.

Finally the grandmother had to ask her son to leave home. Her son remains:

> 'so so about it. He's not so bad, but he still jumps in at [young person] now and then'.

One step-grandparent has lost touch with three of his four children since his wife's grandson moved in. He has grandchildren he has never met. Although, as he pointed out, there is no way he can be sure of their motives, he strongly believes his children are angry and jealous about his commitment to the placement.

> 'They think [name of young person] has taken over'.

5 Supporting kinship care

In this chapter we present carers' and young people's views about the assistance they received and, drawing on social workers' views as well, identify the additional supports needed to sustain and develop kinship care. Immediately prior to and during the research period (2000–01) Wandsworth Social Services Department was subject to reorganisation, budgetary reviews and staff shortages. These matters are not presented as 'excuses' but this context is important in understanding what seemed to the research team as an ongoing unsettled climate, constantly driven by pressing needs and demands exceeding resources.

Support received

Support for the young people

We asked the young people what sort of help and support they had received during and immediately prior to their kinship care placement. The limited support young people and carers received came predominantly from either the social services, the education authority, the family, or a combination of all three. The young people both valued and criticised the type and level of social services support received. All said that they had seen many different social workers, some of whom they had liked, but for some no bonds had been made. The following quotations illustrate the range of opinion:

> 'When I was in the bedsit I had a key worker – they helped me quite a lot. If I needed anything they always knew a way of doing it. So I had a lot of support in the bedsit'.

> 'My social worker, she's helped me through a lot'.

> 'My social worker, he is really lovely, I do have a lot of faith in

> him ... he's helped me a lot and he's very trustworthy, I do feel I can trust him and he has helped me a lot. I think he's only doing it – being a social worker – for a little while'.

> 'My last social worker left, all of my social workers left. My first one he left to go and do something else; my second one she moved, I think she went to another place; my other one moved, they've all moved'.

> 'Social workers, had about four, all useless'.

Some young people spoke of teachers who had helped them through difficult times:

> 'I've always had someone that I could see, like that teacher at my old school, then I had a teacher at the Tech, then ...'

Support for the carers

Given fairly low expectations, carers valued social services when they provided any support at all, since they were also unclear what they were entitled to. Specific requests for help (with finances or education) were met by mixed responses, depending on the social worker. Some social workers received special praise. For example, one had arranged for the carer to receive payments until the young person was 19 so that her longer-term education was assured, organised private tutoring with charitable money so that she could catch up with her studies, arranged child benefit, and organised a replacement birth certificate. Other carers described how helpful their social workers had been when looking for a suitable secondary school for the grandchildren concerned – both had special educational needs. Other positive responses include:

> 'Obviously I'm not her only client and there's loads of children that she's got to deal with, so obviously it's not like I can have her all to myself, you know what I mean. She gives as much support as she can give, but it would be nice at some times to have more support'.

> 'I've had at least five or six social workers, I've got on with every single one'.

In another case a carer gave special praise to a social worker saying that she had always had a soft spot for the young person and 'did everything she could to help him'. In particular:

'I asked for help when [name of young person] was playing up at school. I thought it was my fault that he had changed and didn't want to go to school. The social worker said it was because [name of young person] was growing up. It made me feel better as if I wasn't to blame'.

Almost without exception, carers spoke highly of the support they were receiving or had received from the schools, both from the teaching staff and education social workers. The relationship with the schools was especially critical to these carers. Another key source of support for kinship carers, potentially at least, was that derived from their own family members. Yet the ability of carers to gain support in looking after the young person from other members of the family and friends varied enormously. Around half of the carers described how members of the family provided financial or other material help, for example in providing clothes, help in finding a college place, or looking after the young people on occasion.

Elsewhere however, the carers gave the impression that the responsibility was theirs and theirs alone. Most often this was because the carers felt that it was simply unfair to ask others to get involved, for example two carers said:

'They've all got their own lives to live, their own children to raise'.

'My daughter is working and has a family. This problem is not her responsibility. I would not put pressure on her'.

Sometimes the absence of family support was because the young people made special demands, for example:

'The boys are difficult. It's something they [other members of the family] can't help with. You need a lot of experience to look after them'.

In other cases, as we have seen, family members refused to get involved because they were angry about the caring responsibilities:

'[name of partner]'s side have shown a bit of resentment – I think it's jealousy. They think he has taken over'.

Yet in the main, social services were the main support agency and, as such, they also received some criticisms from carers.

Support needed

Almost all carers wanted more social services support, and better financial support.

Social services support

In relation to social services support, carers wanted more visits, improved and much more consistent communication, and phone contact with social services. For others they would value the opportunity to talk about how to handle family relationship issues: either parenting issues concerning the young person, or wider family relationship issues. Others needed help with accommodation in the light of their expanding family responsibilities. In just one case did a carer argue that a carers' group to 'talk things through' would be helpful. Six carers described problems in getting the help they needed to specific requests. Three carers wanted help in finding daytime activities for the young person. One grandson for example attended school for just one hour each day and, for the rest of the time, he was under his grandmother's feet. She felt she had no way of escaping the responsibility of looking after him. Another wanted help to find a larger home to accommodate her grandson who was sleeping on the floor.

Around half the carers were isolated and felt they were not getting enough support,

> 'They could have come in for a chat now and then ... offer friendliness and encouragement'.

Another said

> 'When I was trying to get in touch with [the social worker] when [the young person] was suspended she wasn't there. I needed help there and then. I wanted to get it all off my chest ... When [social worker] did finally get in touch it was too late'.

Many carers were puzzled when their social worker was not available, that another could not help or be put on the case, one aspect of a case management model (on case management in kinship care, see O'Brien, 2001).

Financial support

The main problems in relation to financial support were the small amounts and inconsistencies in the amounts made available. As one grandparent typically described it,

'It's reasonable to pay grandparents to look after children – they have to take extra responsibilities – children cannot eat without money'.

The arrangements for financial support created most bitterness. Although we did not ask for financial details for this study, some carers volunteered the amounts. The picture looked erratic. One grandparent looking after two grandchildren received £103 every two weeks; a second received £132 a fortnight for one young adult; a third, £190 a month for one young adult; another, a total of £600 over a seven-year period. A previous study in the same local authority also revealed payment variations and reported average weekly payments of £61 per child per week. In that study older children, aged between 11 and 16 years, received higher weekly average amounts of between £80 and £100 (Broad, 1998b). This is a much higher level than for the only other local authority known to have published figures (Webster, 2000: 9) where £50 was the maximum weekly payment and 'contributions from a parent' were also sometimes sought ('even if it amounted to 50p').

Some carers felt they were being exploited because they were 'family' and several pointed out that without their intervention, the costs to social services would be much greater:

'If he was in a home he would be costing them [social services] £200 a week'.

'If you care for a foster child – you don't have all the financial worries blood relatives have'.

The second main problem was inconsistency in relation to both one-off payments and regular fees. One carer for example described how it was possible to get money to pay for a holiday one year, but not the next. A second described how she was not automatically informed that she could get an allowance for her grandson's behavioural problems. This she had to find out herself.

The relationship between carers and financial support from social services was, for some, double-edged. On the one hand, carers recognised that the personal sacrifices they were making enabled social services to save money by avoiding more expensive state care for the young person, and they were seriously in need of financial assistance. On the other, the money came with strings attached, that is social worker intervention. Accepting such support changed the power relationship and the carer became a client. Carers noted the adverse effects of this change of status: they were now expected to attend meetings at times that suited social workers rather than themselves, which disrupted other commitments.

Carers felt that decisions made in relation to one-off grants for, say, holidays and special needs' allowances, were down to chance rather than a coherent policy. Some social workers appeared more generous than others, and the same social worker could be inconsistent over time. The result was that carers couldn't plan their household expenditure over a long term.

Social workers also pointed out that the funding for kinship care was a difficult and emotive subject, for the carers themselves, for social workers and for politicians:

> ' There are also different viewpoints ... about whether you should be paying families or you shouldn't be paying families to look after the relatives. I'm sure social workers have different views on that to the politicians'.

Information

Many carers seemed unsure about their legal position and had fairly low or no expectations of services being available. Many said that they wanted more information about any specialist youth or education services, and financial entitlements.

A gateway to other services

Three carers called for better access to youth provision or specifically for day-time activities for those young people who had either left school, been excluded or who were in partial education. For example:

> 'They could get help, get him involved in sports, clubs ... It's hard to do those things at our age'.

Another carer wanted access to respite care:

> '[name of social worker] said she was trying to get me respite care ... I don't get the help when I get so tired ... when [name of grandson] is so bad'.

Two others wanted help with finding housing – one wanted a larger house for herself and her grandson, and the second wanted help with finding suitable accommodation for her pregnant granddaughter.

More family support for and from birth parents

The grandparents were especially concerned about the well-being of the birth parents and argued that they should get more support. This, they pointed out, would not only help the parents themselves but would benefit the young person as well. For their own caring tasks the support and acknowledgement from their families, birth parents and especially any partners, was an important source of support for them.

> 'When they move a child from the home they should make sure that the parent gets treatment. The mother will always be that child's mother. If the mother is unhappy with the situation or unwell, then the child will suffer'.

A couple of carers also made the point that if the mother had been supported more by social services in the first place, the family may not have got into such difficulties.

The need for policy changes

All local stakeholders considered that kinship care did not have a high enough profile, either at a national level or within the borough. From the social services perspective there were organisational and policy guidance issues highlighted. One recently qualified social worker pointed out, for example, that kinship care hardly featured in his social work training. Another noted that kinship care does not readily fit into the pattern of social work priorities:

> 'I think part of the problem is that we work in a bureaucracy that has to have procedures and so when a child is looked after, we are in no doubt as to what we are expected to do ... I think the challenge of kinship care is that each family we work with is at a different point in that spectrum ... we are not very good as a large organisation looking at the individual needs of the particular kinship carer.'

Some wondered whether this was because it involves a disproportionate amount of black families:

> 'When we look at the amount of black kinship carers in the borough compared to white kinship carers, it shows that it is higher ... I just wonder when the balance changes, whether the borough will change its view, because for black people any time

there's any changes it's usually because the indigenous society
feels that there's more need for them.'

Others felt that the gender of the carers might also contribute to the low profile:

'When you talk about extended families, it's the women who are
the carers. It's unpaid work, it's assumed'.

Many social workers described how difficult it is to support kinship care without a
clear policy framework – as one social worker put it:

'It concerns me because it means that the people out there, the
families, are getting a different service, there's no policy or basis
or value on which those judgements are being made.'

6 Discussion and recommendations

Introduction

Young people who have had an unstable upbringing, who have experienced neglect and periods looked after by the local authority, and who can no longer live with their birth parent(s) have an especially powerful need to feel safe and secure, be listened to and accepted for who they are. The young people in this study have had some or all of those background experiences and highly valued living with their extended family in kinship care. The carers, most of whom were grandparents, had a commitment to caring, as a natural loving response. They also had a desire to prevent 'their' child from being taken away from the family. They were frightened of what might happen if the young person went into public care, and what would happen when they were forced to leave.

Discussion

Policy invisibility

One of the problems facing this group of young people is that in policy terms they are largely 'invisible' in that they do not neatly fit into existing Department of Health administrative classifications. It will be recalled that in recognition of that problem, the research team requested the local authority to add a new 'kinship' field to a children 'in need' database. Children and young people in kinship care placements do not necessarily fit into the legal categories of being looked after or, as a sub-set of looked after, placed in foster care. Also many, but not all, of the young people in this study were subject to Residence Orders. Given the extent and use of formal kinship care placements (whether or not fostered with a relative or friend) there is an urgent need to make this group more visible in policy terms. It is suggested here that only by doing this will it be likely that support and guidance will develop.

Opening the floodgates

It is also likely that some local authorities will take the view that if they are seen as supporting some family placements this will, as one local authority officer put it, 'open the floodgates'. In other words if they encourage kinship care placements they will then be expected to fund them. This stance seems unnecessarily defensive in the sense that local authorities could introduce payment thresholds, but it indicates a perceived if not an actual barrier.

Entitlements and discretion

Another key issue concerns the balance between flexibility and clarity in respect of financial entitlements and welfare supports. For example there is a financial policy in Wandsworth Social Services Department about payment levels to kinship carers. Thus there seems to be clarity. However the carers and social workers alike felt constrained by this policy when discussing 'case by case' needs which normally exceeded the amounts allowed. Yet without any policy being in place, some kinship carers may have been assessed as not being entitled to any, or low levels of, financial support. The same 'entitlements or discretion' argument also applies to levels of social work support for kinship carers and young people. Wide consultation and an agreement about setting national kinship care standards would help here.

Service delivery

Reiterating the finding that social services found it difficult to prioritise kinship care support services, in part because of their other statutory protection duties, it is therefore especially important to draw attention to a different kinship care service delivery approach, one based in New Zealand. There it is the voluntary sector which undertakes family support work (including kinship care) rather than the statutory social services departments which focus more on child protection duties. Thus kinship care support services are delivered by voluntary organisations funded by the state. Additionally there is an entitlement to an allowance for any child living in kinship care. This is called the 'unattached child allowance' and is payable by the Department of Social Security (not social services) to a child living in kinship care. This allowance is paid to the child and is attached to the child rather than the carer and is at foster care allowance levels. This approach might meet some of the carers' concerns expressed here.

Love and emotional permanence

A sense of 'emotional permanence', feeling safe and secure living within their extended family, which many of the young people expressed, resulted directly from the family love they received and, was not related to whether or not any legal order was in place.

Ethnicity and kinship care

Fifty-eight per cent of the young people and kinship carers in this study were of Caribbean, Guyanese or African ethnic origin. There was evidence of more widespread extended family support being provided above and beyond grandparents, by sisters and aunts in these minority ethnic families. Research from North America also suggests that kinship care is more common among black and Hispanic children (Clarke and Cairns, 2001). Kinship care arrangements demonstrate the potential for reinforcing racial identity and feelings of belonging. This was linked to two important factors: the first was living within an extended family network; and the second was having frequent and liberal contact.

Recommendations

Clarity and agreement about the term 'kinship care'

This study provided a working definition of the term 'kinship care' and there is emerging evidence that the term is becoming more widely used and accepted. Nevertheless there may still be a need for explicit agreement across the whole UK about the term to be used to describe formal kinship care placements.

Kinship care policies

- *Management information* — While the Department of Health does publish information about relative foster care and other non-relative foster care, and about looked after children and those children on Residence Orders, this information excludes the majority of those in this study who are not looked after but who are young people in need in kinship care, and who are subject to a range of administrative dispositions. Residence Order returns to the Department of Health may also be incomplete and may not contain the level of detail about kinship care placements required. This lack of separate information on the nature, extent and use of kinship care is also a feature of many international child welfare systems (Gleeson, 1996). This makes it very difficult to track precisely the rate at which change is taking place. It is therefore recommended that kinship care information be more systematically gathered.

- *A placement or an arrangement?* — There is a fundamental question which underlines the definitional and status ambiguity of kinship care: is it a formal placement or an arrangement between relatives and friends? We would argue that within the terms of our definition, because most of the children and young people are in need and social services have become involved, that kinship care is a formal placement and therefore should usually be regarded as such by social services departments.

- *The scope of kinship care* — There is emerging evidence from the Department of Health and social services departments that kinship care placements, whether relative foster care and other family and friends care, are increasing. This is largely as a result of initiatives by social services resulting from a shortage of other suitable placement options. However while such expansion of provision might be welcome, further research is recommended to explore whether kinship care placements initiated by local authorities, rather than those initiated by extended family members, are always appropriate. In other words it could be the case that if social services were encouraged to expand levels of kinship care provision, more risks might be taken about the suitability and/or appropriateness of all those placements. It is acknowledged that a comprehensive assessment framework would help to assess suitability and reduce the risk of placement breakdown (on assessment see Pitcher, 2001).

- *Cross cutting policies* — Social services departments primarily provide welfare support; they are not income maintenance agencies. It is recommended that the Department of Health has inter-departmental or 'joined-up' discussions with the Treasury, Department of Social Security and Inland Revenue to explore whether tax credits or grants might be introduced for kinship carers.

- *Guidance* — It is recommended here that the Department of Health issues guidance about the use of formal kinship care placements with a proviso that where kinship care placements are not just considered, but pursued, they are properly funded and supported in an active partnership with the young person, extended family and carers.

- *Finances* — This study shows a need for local authorities to develop strategies for supporting and helping kinship carers who may struggle to support children.

Realistic financial assistance should be given in order to help families in a meaningful way.

- *The contribution of kinship care* — Local authorities should begin to recognise the contribution that kinship care makes in the lives of children who cannot remain with their parents and, in appropriate cases, value it as a viable alternative to stranger foster care. Specialist private residential placements for children can cost anything between £1000 and £3000 per week. In our earlier study in the same local authority the kinship carers received on average £61 per week (Broad, 2001b) and there was no evidence from this study to show that these levels had changed.

- *Service delivery* — There is a strong case here for recommending that the voluntary sector takes the lead in delivering appropriate kinship care services that are sensitive and responsive to users' and carers' needs. This would need to be funded by central government and could be delivered in partnership with, or separately from, social services departments and other agencies. As we highlighted earlier in this chapter this is similar to the care service delivery model used in New Zealand. It is recommended that the New Zealand model of service delivery and financial support is worth exploring further within the UK context.

Kinship care practice

- *Assessment* — Kinship care should be subject to a formal assessment but this need not be as comprehensive as a foster care assessment (BAAF, Form F). In this way the purpose and scope of the assessment will be transparent and assessments should become more consistent.

- *Placement options* — Professionals need to explore the options open to children in need and then act positively by giving kinship care equal weighting within the decision making process.

- *Schooling* —Young people in kinship care often face difficulties in school and with their health and/or behaviour. These problems need to be identified so that appropriate support can be provided.

- *Working across boundaries* — Better ways need to be identified to engage in good practice across local authority boundaries so that carers outside the immediate local authority can be better supported.

- *Partnerships* — The notion of shared care between families and social services requires that both agree the nature of these partnerships.

- *Who looks after the needs of carers?* — It is strongly recommended that a policy framework for non-fostering kinship carers is developed and costed in consultation with kinship carers, in order for a dedicated and comprehensive kinship care placement support service to be provided.

- *Access to services* — It is essential that carers and young people gain access to other services, especially respite care, more social work support, education support services, after school services and youth services.

- *Entitlements and support* — Kinship carers often did not know if they were entitled to any financial or other support. Although carers would not have wanted to stop providing love and care, even without any additional support, in some cases their health appeared to be affected.

Further research

As we saw earlier, the current legislation (Children Act 1989, S.23, para 6) encourages placement of the child with a person connected with that child, for example, a family member or friend. We do not know from this research in what proportion of a local authority's cases a placement with a member of the extended family was fully considered and whether the reasons for such decisions were made clear. It would be valuable to obtain this information.

There is also a need for more research in the UK on users' and carers' views, and on the outcomes of kinship care compared with other care placements.

Conclusion

For most of the 50 young people at the centre of this research study, living with an extended family member is a loving, highly valued and secure experience. This seemed to be largely as a result of the young person and their carer's loving commitment to each other and wanting their relationship to work. It is also the case that fear of being placed (back) into care was another motivating factor. It is our view that kinship carers should not 'suffer in silence' about their unmet needs and that more consistent emotional and practical support should be offered. Without such support, there is a serious risk that a number of these predominantly stable kinship care placements will 'break down' sooner or later with all the unnecessary consequences and suffering that can follow.

The evidence presented here suggests that for most of the young people, living in kinship care provides a high measure of personal stability, and a continuity and stability of family relationships and cultural identity severed by previous placements. A strong case has been presented for urging local authorities, the voluntary sector and central government to rise to the challenge of supporting children and young people in need living in kinship care much more that has been the case to date. This will first require a policy debate and agreement about the place and purpose of kinship care. Only then is it likely that children and young people in need and their kinship carers will be sufficiently valued and prioritised to receive the levels of emotional, practical and financial supports needed.

References

Ahmed, A (1990) *Black Perspectives in Social Work Practice.* Venture Press

Aldgate, J (1991) Partnership with parents – fantasy or reality, *Adoption and Fostering,* 15, 2, 1–10

Barn, R (1991) *Black Children in the Public Care System.* Batsford

Berridge, D (1985) *Children's Homes.* Basil Blackwell

Berridge, D (1987) *Foster Care: a Research Review.* The Stationary Office

Berridge, D and Brodie, I (1997) *Children's Homes Revisited.* Jessica Kingsley

Berridge, D and Cleaver, H (1987) *Foster Home Breakdown.* Basil Blackwell

Biehal N and others (1995) *Moving On.* HMSO

Biehal, N, Clayden J and Byford, S (2000) *Home or Away? Supporting Young People and Families.* National Children's Bureau/Joseph Rowntree Foundation

Broad, B (1998a) *Young People Leaving Care.* Jessica Kingsley

Broad, B (1998b) *Child Placements with Relatives and Friends – final report,* mimeo, London Borough of Wandsworth Social Services Department

Broad, B (1999a) Kinship care: enabling and supporting child placements with relatives and friends *in Assessment, Preparation and Support.* BAAF, 77–85

Broad, B (1999b) Kinship Care: children and young people placed with extended families or friends, *Childright,* 155, 16–17

Broad, B (ed.) (2001a) *Kinship Care: the Placement of Choice for Children and Young People.* Russell House Publishing

Broad, B (2001b) Kinship care: supporting children in extended family and friends placements, *Adoption and Fostering,* 25, 2, 1–9

Broad, B and Saunders, L (1998) Involving young people leaving care as peer researchers in a health research project: a learning experience, *Research, Policy and Planning,* 16, 1, 1–19

Child Welfare League of America (1994) *Kinship Care: a Natural Bridge.* Washington DC: CWLA

Clarke, L and Cairns, H (2001) 'Grandparents and the care of children: the research evidence' *in* Broad, B (ed.) 2001a *op. cit.*

Denscombe, M (1998) *The Good Research Guide.* Open University Press

DoH (1990) *The Care of Children – Principles and Practice in Regulations and Guidance.* HMSO

DoH (1991) *The Children Act 1989 Guidance and Regulations.* Volume Three. Department of Health

DoH (1995) *The Children Act 1989 Residence Orders Study.* Department of Health, Social Services Inspectorate

DoH (1997) *People Like Us*. Sir William Utting. Department of Health

DoH (1998a) *The Health of Children Looked After, Report of the Department of Health Select Committee*. Department of Health

DoH (1998b) *Quality Protects: Transforming Children's Services*. Department of Health

DoH (1999) *Children Looked After by Local Authorities Year Ending 31 March 1998*. Department of Health

DoH (2000a) Quality Protects Placement Choice seminar, 12 January 2000. Department of Health

DoH (2000b) *Framework for the Assessment of Children in Need and Their Families*. Department of Health

DoH (2000c) *Tracking Progress in Children's Services: an Evaluation of Local Responses to the Quality Protects Programme,* year 2 National Overview Report. Department of Health

DoH (2000d) *Planning and Providing Good Quality Placements for Children in Care*. Department of Health

DoH (2001) *Children Looked After by Local Authorities Year Ending 31 March 2000*. Department of Health

Fisher, M and others (1986) *In and Out of Care: the Experiences of Children, Parents and Social Workers*. Batsford

Flynn, R (2000) 'Kinship foster care', *Highlight no 179*. National Children's Bureau

Gilligan, R (1997) Beyond permanence: the importance of resilience in child practice and planning, *Adoption and Fostering*, 20, 2

Gleeson, J P (1996) Kinship Care as a Child Welfare Service: The Policy Debate in an Era of Welfare Reform, *Child Welfare,* 75, 419–49

Graham, M (1999) The African-Centred World View: Developing a Paradigm for Social Work, *British Journal of Social Work*, 250–63

Greeff, R *ed.* (1998) *Kinship Care: An International Perspective*. Avebury

Health Development Agency (2000) *Changing Families, Changing Communities*. Health Development Agency

Hill, M (1999) 'Introduction' *in* Hill, M *ed. Signposts in Fostering: Policy, Practice and Research Issues*. BAAF, 2–10

Home Office (1998) *Supporting Families: A Consultation Document*. Home Office

Ince, L 'Promoting kinship foster care: preserving family networks for black children of African origins' *in* Broad, B *ed.* (2001a) *op. cit.,* 135–46

Jackson, S and Thomas, N (1999) *What Works in Creating Stability for Looked After Children*. Barnados

Katz, L (1996) Permanency action through concurrent planning, *Adoption and Fostering,* 20, 2, 8–13

Kent, P, Pierson, J and Thornton, B (1990) Guide to the Children Act 1989, *Community Care,* 19, April 1990

Laws, S and Broad, B (2000) *Looking After Children Within the Extended Family: Carers' Views*. Leicester: Centre for Social Action, De Montfort University 2000

Marsh, P (1998) Leaving care and extended families, *Adoption and Fostering,* 22, 4, 6–14

McClone, F and Smith, K (1998) *Families and Kinship*. Family Policy Studies Centre

McFadden, E J (1998) Kinship Care in the United States, *Adoption and Fostering*, 22, 3, 7–15

McFadden, E J and Downs, S W (1995) Family continuity: the new paradigm in permanency planning, *Community Alternatives*, 7, 1

Murphy, M (1998) Foster parents before relatives, *Social Work Today,* 22, September

National Foster Care Association (1993) 'Friends and Relatives as Carers', Making it Work: 30–33, NFCA

National Foster Care Association (1997) *Foster Care in Crisis.* NFCA

National Foster Care Association (2000) *Family and Friends Carers' Handbook.* NFCA

O'Brien, V 'Contributions from an Irish study: understanding and managing relative care' *in* Broad, B *ed.* (2001a) *op. cit.,* 59–72

Pitcher, D (2001) 'Assessing grandparent carers' *in* Broad, B *ed.* (2001a) *op. cit.,* 105–14

Quality Protects rings the changes, *Community Care,* 2–8 November 2000.

Rashid, S (2000) The strengths of black families appropriate placements for all, A*doption and Fostering,* 24, 1, 15–22

Richards, A and Ince, L (2000) *'Overcoming the Obstacles' looked after children: quality services for Black and minority ethnic children and their families.* Family Rights Group

Rowe, J and others (1984) *Long Term Foster Care.* Batsford

Rowe, J, Hundleby, M and Garnett, L (1989) *Child Care Now: A Survey of Placement Patterns.* BAAF

Save the Children (1995) *You're on Your Own, Young People's Research on Leaving Care.* Save the Children

Sinclair, R, Garnett, L, Berridge, D (1995) Social Work and Assessment with Adolescents, National Children's Bureau

Sinclair, R, Hearn, B and Pugh, G (1997) *Preventive Work with Families: the role of mainstream services.* National Children's Bureau

Thoburn, J (1996) 'The research evidence of the importance of links with relatives when children are in care' in *The Children Act 1989 What's in it for grandparents*? Grandparents' Federation

Triseliotis, J, Borland, M and Hill, M (2000) *Delivering Foster Care.* BAAF

Tunnard, J and Thoburn, J (1997) *The Grandparents' Supporters Project.* University of East Anglia/Grandparents' Federation

Walby, C and Colton, M 'More Children – More Problems?', *Community Care,* 15–21, July 1999

Wandsworth, London Borough of (1996) *Accommodation and placement with relatives and friends,* children and families manual, mimeo. London Borough of Wandsworth

Wandsworth, London Borough of (1997a) *Children Looked After.* London Borough of Wandsworth Social Services Department

Wandsworth, London Borough of (1997b) *Race Record Keeping Analysis.* London Borough of Wandsworth Social Services Department

Wandsworth, London Borough of (1998) *Financial Issues – Child Placement with Relatives and Friends,* mimeo. London Borough of Wandsworth

Waterhouse, S *'Keeping children in kinship placements within court proceedings' in* Broad, B *ed.* (2001a) *op. cit.*

Webster, G (2000) *Use of kinship placements in Hertfordshire,* mimeo. Hertfordshire Social Services Department

Who Cares? Trust (1998) *Remember my messages.* Who Cares? Trust

Index